STANDARDS OF GOOD PRACTICE FOR EDUCATION ABROAD

Sixth Edition

Enhanced edition, including the *Code of Ethics for Education Abroad*

The Forum on Education Abroad

Carlisle, Pennsylvania, USA

The *Standards of Good Practice for Education Abroad*, published by The Forum on Education Abroad, are the only standards established by the Standards Development Organization (SDO) for the field of education abroad recognized by the US Department of Justice and the Federal Trade Commission. For more information, visit www.forumea.org/standards.

ISBN: 978-1-952376-24-5 (paperback)
doi.org/10.36366/S.978-1-952376-24-5

Standards of Good Practice for Education Abroad, Sixth Edition
ISBN: 978-1-95236-02-3 (ebook)
doi.org/10.36366/S.978-1-95236-02-3

Code of Ethics for Education Abroad, Third Edition
ISBN: 978-1-952376-08-5 (ebook)
DOI: doi.org/10.36366/G.978-1-952376-08-5

Library of Congress Control Number: 2020934167

First Printing, 2020.
Second Printing, enhanced edition, 2022.
Third Printing, 2023.

The Forum on Education Abroad
PO Box 1773
Carlisle, PA, USA 17013

The Forum on Education Abroad is hosted by Dickinson College.

www.forumea.org

STANDARDS OF GOOD PRACTICE FOR EDUCATION ABROAD

Enhanced Sixth Edition

INTRODUCTION

This document, published by The Forum on Education Abroad, specifies minimum requirements, quality indicators, and a framework for continuous improvement for education abroad. It is applicable to undergraduate, graduate, professional, and continuing education, whether for credit or not for credit.

The Forum on Education Abroad is recognized by the US Department of Justice and the Federal Trade Commission as the Standards Development Organization (SDO) for the field of education abroad. As such, it is The Forum's responsibility to monitor changes in our field of professional practice and to maintain, update, and promulgate the *Standards of Good Practice for Education Abroad* accordingly.

REVISING THE STANDARDS

During the fall of 2018, The Forum's Standards Manager and the Chair of the Forum Council formed the Standards Update Working Group. The Forum intentionally selected members to represent voices from diverse regions, institution and organization types, and constituents. The Forum released a Notification of Standards Development on October 11, 2018. To ensure even wider and more diverse representation, The Forum hosted a series of online listening sessions over the next six months, scheduled at different times of day. One listening session happened at The Forum's European Conference in Prague, Czech Republic, in October 2018, and another at The Forum's Annual Conference in Denver, Colorado, USA, in March 2019. The Forum collected information from any constituents who could not attend the listening sessions via a submission form available on the organization's website.

The Forum aligned the revision process with the core principles of due process for standards development as identified by the American National Standards Institute (ANSI): Openness, Lack of Dominance, Balance, Coordination and Harmonization, Consideration of View and Objections, Consensus, and Appeals. This included a public comment period on the first draft of the 6th Edition and the formation of a Consensus Body with a diverse membership. In this way, persons directly or materially affected by the *Standards* had the opportunity to have their voices heard in this important process.

After two rounds of voting and revision, consensus (42 affirmative votes; 1 negative vote) was reached by the Consensus Body on October 18, 2019. Following the appeals period, the 6th edition of the Standards of Good Practice for Education Abroad takes effect July 1, 2020.

ACKNOWLEDGMENTS

The Forum thanks the members of the Standards Update Working Group for their outstanding work in preparing the revisions represented in this edition:

Emily Gorlewski, *Wesleyan University, chair*

Abbiola Ballah, *Toucan Education Programs Limited, Belize*

Jennifer Betz, *Piedmont College*

Mieke Berg, *FIE: Foundation for International Education, United Kingdom*

Joy Carew, *University of Louisville*

Theresa Castillo, *Pellissippi State Community College*

Amelia Dietrich, *The Forum on Education Abroad*

Nico Evers, *EARTH University, Costa Rica*

Jessica Francis, *Wake Forest University*

Erin French, *Iowa State University*

Elizabeth Frohlich, *The Forum on Education Abroad*

Anne Haberkern, *Portland Community College*

Cheryl Lochner-Wright, *University of Wisconsin-Eau Claire*

James Lucas, *Michigan State University*

Gareth McFeely, *Boston University*

Natalie A. Mello, *The Forum on Education Abroad, Standards Manager*

Sylvia Mitterndorfer, *William & Mary*

Kevin Murphy, *University of New Haven, Tuscany Campus, Italy*

Heidi Piper, *Griffith University, Australia*

Craig Rinker, *Georgetown University*

David Wick, *Middlebury Institute of International Studies*

As part of the process to update the *Standards of Good Practice for Education Abroad*, the Consensus Body is responsible for voting to approve proposed revisions to the *Standards of Good Practice for Education Abroad* and voting to reaffirm the *Standards of Good Practice for Education Abroad*.

The Forum thanks the following individuals for their service on the Consensus Body for the 2019–2024 term:

Lindsay Allen, *Yale-NUS College, Singapore*

Rosa Almoguera, *Edualamo, Spain*

Alejandra Barahona, *Universidad Veritas CIPSS, Costa Rica*

Heidi Barends, *EDU Africa, South Africa*

Sarah Beaton, *Advanced Training and Research Division, US Department of Education*

Tracey Bradley, *Tennessee Consortium for International Studies/Pellissippi State Community College & Forum Council*

Paige Butler, *Middlebury Institute for International Studies*

Enda Carroll, *University College Dublin & Forum Board of Directors*

Christina Carroll, *Florida State University & Forum Council*

Lucía Conte, *Universitat Pompeu Fabra, Spain*

Christopher Daniel, *Michigan State University*

Rebecca Davies, *University of Dallas*

Pauline Day, *Wellesley College alumna*

Caroline Donovan White, *NAFSA*

Maria Doyle, *University of West Georgia*

Maritheresa Frain, *The Institute for Study Abroad*

Annalease Gibson, *Albany State University*

Robert Hallworth, *IES Abroad & Forum Council*

Kathleen Head, *Elmhurst College*

Kimberly Hindbjorgen, *University of Minnesota*

Holly Hudson, *Texas A&M University*

Heilwig Jones, *Kaya Responsible Travel*

ACKNOWLEDGMENTS

Jonathan Kaplan, *Rothberg International School, The Hebrew University of Jerusalem*

Arden Kazan, *CISAbroad – Center for International Studies*

Sophia Krause, *Freie Universität Berlin International Summer and Winter University (FUBiS), Germany*

Sarah Langston Urbiss, *SAI Programs*

John Lucas, *ISEP – International Student Exchange Programs & Forum Board of Directors*

Blaise Maccarrone, *CIEE*

Monica Malhotra, *Mobility International*

Alex Markman, *Universidad Torcuato Di Tella, Argentina*

Amanda Milburn, *Global Education Oregon in London*

Jennifer Murray, *Bard College*

Michael Nelson, *University of Illinois at Urbana-Champaign*

Ken Nesbett, *Kirkwood Community College*

Carri Orrison, *Global Experiences*

Clare Overman, *Institute of International Education (IIE)*

James Pasquill, *State University of New York*

Chris Petrie, *Eastern Florida State College*

Pia Schneider, *Iowa State University & EUASA*

Gregory Spear, *Georgetown University*

Tynelle Stewart, *University of Rochester & Forum Council*

Ann Margaret Themistocleous, *Anderson University*

Brigette Thompson, *AIFS Study Abroad*

Jill Walker, *Global Vision International (GVI), Thailand*

The Forum also thanks the individuals who shared their feedback and suggestions throughout the period of information-gathering and during the public comment period.

HOW TO USE THE STANDARDS

The *Standards of Good Practice for Education Abroad* can be used as a tool to:

- guide program development,

- evaluate program quality,

- advocate for resources and support,

- train new professionals,

- educate stakeholders such as parents, faculty, students, etc.,

- establish and maintain respectful, sustainable relationships between partners.

While these *Standards* represent consensus in the field of education abroad at the postsecondary level, other constituents may find the *Standards* useful for informing their own practices. These groups may include primary and secondary educators providing education abroad programs to their own students and institutions and organizations offering education abroad programs for participants from countries other than the US.

The number and order of the clauses that follow do not imply hierarchy, importance, or a suggested order of operations. Use these *Standards* holistically.

Throughout the *Standards*, use this guide established by the International Organization for Standardization (ISO), to understand the expectations set by each clause [1]:

- **shall** indicates minimum requirements

- **should** indicates recommendations

- **can** indicates further possibilities for improvement

Definitions of frequently used and field-specific terms are provided in Section 3 for reference. In some cases, common words have been defined in order to ensure a shared understanding of how these words are used within the context of these *Standards of Good Practice* and to make the document accessible to readers who may have learned English as a second or foreign language.

Sections 4, 5, and 6 comprise the clauses and subclauses, the core of the Standards. Section 4 outlines guiding principles, which should be thought of as overarching and applying to the next two sections. Section 5 deals with the administrative framework for education abroad, and Section 6 deals with student learning and development, further divided into considerations for the phases before, during, and after study abroad participation. The Standards Update Working Group developed this structure to speak more directly to individuals, institutions, and organizations in many contexts and with varied influence or responsibility over the education abroad process. The structure lends itself to holistic use, rather than to a more fragmented approach, in which users choose discrete chunks of the *Standards* to focus on because those are the ones they consider to be in their purview.

Those who are accustomed to using previous versions of the *Standards*, or those who are looking for guidance on certain topics, will find the topical index in the Annex useful. For example, someone who is looking for information on health, safety, security, and risk management will find these topics not on their own in one particular section, but woven throughout Sections 4, 5, and 6. The index will give the specific clause(s) and/or subclause(s) where each topic may be found. The index will allow users to find specific information incorporated within the holistic *Standards* structure.

1. SCOPE

This document specifies minimum requirements, quality indicators, and a framework for continuous improvement for education abroad. It applies to undergraduate, graduate, professional, and continuing education, whether for credit or not for credit.

2. NORMATIVE REFERENCE

The following document is referred to in the text in such a way that some or all of its content constitutes requirements of this document. For an undated reference, the latest edition of the referenced document (including any amendments) applies.

Code of Ethics for Education Abroad (The Forum on Education Abroad) https://forumea.org/resources/standards-of-good-practice/code-of-ethics/

3. TERMS AND DEFINITIONS

3.1. ASSESS

measure effectiveness through the articulation of *goals* (3.17), development of associated measures, and identification of observable outputs and *outcomes* (3.29, 3.30)

3.2. ASSESSMENT

process of measuring effectiveness, usually through the articulation of *goals* (3.17) and performance measures, the development of associated measures, and the identification of observable *outcomes* (3.29, 3.30)

Note 1 to entry: Assessment is usually used to inform whether the initial goals were achieved.

3.3. CO-CURRICULAR

relating to activities or events that complement or enhance *curricular* (3.9) *goals* (3.17)

Note 1 to entry: Co-curricular activities are typically non-academic in nature but relate other activities and experiences to the established curriculum or pedagogy.

3.4. CONTINUING EDUCATION

education available to adult, part-time *students* (3.45)

3.5. COURSE

unit of instruction

Note 1 to entry: In this document, course does not refer to a full degree program.

3.6. CREDIT

unit that colleges and universities use to record the successful completion of *courses* (3.5)

3.7. CREDIT TRANSFER

process by which *credit* (3.6) earned during *education abroad* (3.11) is transferred, approved, accepted, or otherwise validated by the *institution* (3.24) from which a student is seeking a degree

3.8. CRITICAL INCIDENT

any actual or alleged event or situation that creates a significant risk of substantial or serious harm to the physical or mental health, safety, or well-being of a *participant* (3.31) that requires a response by program *personnel* (3.34) or first responders, or an event that prevents a *participant* (3.31) from successful participation in the *program* (3.40)

Note 1 to entry: This definition is adapted from the North Dakota Department of Human Services Medical Services Division. [2]

Note 2 to entry: Critical incidents under this definition should not be confused with critical incidents in education, which refer more generally to experiences which cause stress and can serve as "teaching moments."

3.9. CURRICULAR

relating to expectations and requirements for a program of study

3.10. DIVERSITY

individual differences (e.g., personality, learning styles, and life experiences) and group/social differences (e.g., race/ethnicity, class, gender, sexual orientation, country of origin, and ability, as well as cultural, political, religious, or other affiliations)

Note 1 to entry: This definition is by the Association of American Colleges and Universities (AAC&U). [3]

3.11. EDUCATION ABROAD

education, including, but not limited to, enrollment in courses, experiential learning, internships, service learning, and other learning activities, which occurs outside the participant's home country, the country in which they are enrolled as a student, or the country in which they are employed as *personnel* (3.34)

Note 1 to entry: Education abroad does not, in itself, result in a degree.

3.12. EQUITABLE

having or exhibiting *equity* (3.13); characterized by fairness; just and right; reasonable

3.13. EQUITY

creation of opportunities for historically underrepresented populations to have equal access to and participate in educational programs that are capable of closing the achievement gaps

Note 1 to entry: Adapted from the Association of American Colleges & Universities (AAC&U). [3]

3.14. ETHICS

moral principles that govern a person's behavior or how an activity is conducted

Note 1 to entry: As defined by the Oxford Dictionaries. [4]

3.15. EVALUATION

critical examination involving interpretation and judgment related to effectiveness and quality

3.16. FACULTY

person or people who teach *postsecondary* (3.37) *courses* (3.5)

Note 1 to entry: Faculty members may include all types of professors and instructors, regardless of tenure or type of contract.

3.17. GOAL

the final or ultimate aim towards which efforts are directed

Note 1 to entry: Achieving a goal will involve the development of a clear implementation plan of intermediary steps, each designed to build on elements of that goal.

3.18. GUIDELINE

general rule, principle, or piece of advice

Note 1 to entry: As defined by Oxford Dictionaries. [4]

3.19. HISTORICALLY UNDERREPRESENTED

African American, American Indian/Alaska Native, and Latino students who have historically comprised a minority of the US population

3.20. HISTORICALLY UNDERSERVED

populations of students who have not been recruited to participate in study or education abroad, including, but not limited to, LGBTQ+ students, students of color, undocumented students, non-traditionally aged students, and first generation students

3.21. IDENTITY

who a person is, or the qualities of a person or group that make them different from others

Note 1 to entry: As defined by the Cambridge Dictionary. [5]

3.22. INCLUSION

active, intentional, and ongoing engagement with *diversity* (3.10) —in the curriculum, in the co-curriculum, and in communities (intellectual, social, cultural, geographical) with which individuals might connect—in ways that increase awareness, content knowledge, cognitive sophistication, and empathic understanding of the complex ways individuals interact within systems and institutions

Note 1 to entry: As defined by the Association of American Colleges and Universities (AAC&U). [3]

3.23. INCLUSIVE

intentionally engaging with *diversity* (3.10)

Note 1 to entry: See also: *inclusion* (3.22).

3.24. INSTITUTION

entity that provides education as its main purpose, including, but not limited to, a school, college, university, or training center

Note 1 to entry: Such institutions are often accredited or sanctioned by the relevant national, regional, or discipline-specific education authorities or equivalent authorities. Educational institutions may also be operated by private organizations, including, but not limited to, religious bodies, special interest groups, or private educational and training enterprises, both for-profit and non-profit.

Note 2 to entry: Adapted from the UNESCO Institute for Statistics. [6]

Note 3 to entry: An institution may be referred to as an *organization* (3.28), but not all organizations are institutions.

3.25. LOCAL COMMUNITY

community in which an *education abroad* (3.11) *participant* (3.31) lives and learns

3.26. NOT FOR CREDIT

coursework or *co-curricular* (3.3) activities for which students do not earn academic *credit* (3.6)

3.27. OBJECTIVE

specific, measurable result used to work towards *goals* (3.17) and achieve measurable *outcomes* (3.29, 3.30)

Note 1 to entry: Objectives can be thought of as steps that are taken to achieve a broader *goal* (3.17).

3.28. ORGANIZATION

entity involved in providing *education abroad* (3.11) *programs* (3.40)

Note 1 to entry: An institution may be referred to as an organization, but not all organizations are institutions.

Note 2 to entry: A smaller part of an institution or organization, including an education abroad office or a global programs division, may be referred to as an organization.

3.29. OUTCOME, PROGRAM/PROGRAMMATIC

a measure of the results of a *program* (3.40) or service-level *goal* (3.17), e.g., increased satisfaction, increased retention

Note 1 to entry: Program outcomes are often used to include operational outcomes, which represent elements of the program's functioning (e.g., cost per student).

Note 2 to entry: Adapted from the Council for the Advancement of Standards, Glossary of Terms. [7]

3.30. OUTCOME, STUDENT LEARNING

statement which describes significant and measurable change occurring in students as a direct result of their interaction with an *organization* (3.28) and its *programs* (3.40) and services

3.31. PARTICIPANT

individual who attends, provides, or teaches an education abroad *program* (3.40), including, but not limited to:

- program administrator
- on-site faculty/staff
- learner

3.32. PARTNER

party involved in the processes of sending *students* (3.45) abroad or receiving students abroad (when at least two parties are involved), including, but not limited to:

- home institution
- host institution
- independent provider
- consortium
- travel or logistics provider
- government agency
- scholarship organization

Note 1 to entry: Education abroad is by its very nature collaborative. Partner relationships are not always formal partnerships but working relationships with entities that may include, but are not limited to, travel agents or local transportation providers.

3.33. PARTNERSHIP

a formal or informal agreement between two or more *responsible organizations* (3.42) to manage and operate *education abroad* (3.11) *programs* (3.40)

Note 1 to entry: Partnerships may also be formal or informal agreements with vendors for provision of goods or services involved in the management or logistics of *education abroad* (3.11) *programs* (3.40).

3.34. PERSONNEL

individual(s) with responsibility for any aspect of the *portfolio* (3.36) or *program* (3.40), including, but not limited to:

- full-time and/or part-time *faculty* (3.16)
- hourly employees
- administrators
- staff
- paraprofessionals (e.g., student employees, interns, graduate assistants, and volunteers)

3.35. POLICY

plan to address anticipated conditions that guides and determines present and future decisions and acceptable *procedures* (3.38), including, but not limited to:

- reimbursement for early withdrawal
- student conduct
- admissions

3.36. PORTFOLIO OF PROGRAMS

set of experiences that include all specific *programs* (3.40) offered or approved by a *responsible organization* (3.42)

3.37. POSTSECONDARY

educational level following the completion of a school providing a secondary education, including, but not limited to, a high school, secondary school, university-preparatory school, gymnasium, home schooling at the secondary level, or General Education Development (GED)

Note 1 to entry: Also known as higher or tertiary education, postsecondary education is in the US taken to include undergraduate and postgraduate education. Colleges, universities, institutes of technology, and polytechnics are the main institutions that provide postsecondary education.

Note 2 to entry: Adapted from USLegal. [8]

3.38. PROCEDURES

a set way of doing something driven by the completion of a task with a focus on satisfying the rules, for example, in the event of:

- emergency evacuation
- response to sexual misconduct
- termination from internship site

Note 1 to entry: Adapted from ISO Terms Definitions. [9]

3.39. PROCESS

a series of actions completed to achieve a desired outcome, including, but not limited to:

- enrollment
- internship placement
- withdrawal

Note 1 to entry: Adapted from ISO Terms Definitions. [9]

3.40. PROGRAM

specific *education abroad* (3.11) experience, including, but not limited to:

- regular offering of a faculty-led or instructor-led experience
- ongoing direct exchange opportunity
- regular offering of a host institution abroad
- internship opportunity
- service learning experience

3.41. REASONABLE ACCOMMODATIONS

modification or adjustment to a course, program, service, job, activity, assessment, test, or facility that enables a qualified individual with a disability to have equal opportunity to attain the same level of performance or to enjoy the same benefits and privileges that are available to an individual without a disability

Note 1 to entry: As defined in Higher Education Law. [10]

3.42. RESPONSIBLE ORGANIZATION

entity responsible for the execution of a *program* (3.40) or *portfolio of programs* (3.36), including, but not limited to:

- university
- college
- program provider organization
- *partner* (3.32)
- education abroad office
- professional school
- academic department
- career services office

Note 1 to entry: The responsible organization may be different for each program or institution.

Note 2 to entry: See also *organization* (3.28) and *institution* (3.24).

3.43. RESPONSIBLE PARTY

individual responsible for specific task or *program* (3.40), including, but not limited to:

- advisor
- program leader
- education abroad director
- risk manager

Note 1 to entry: The responsible party may be different for each task or program.

3.44. RESTORATIVE JUSTICE

a philosophy that focuses on repairing the harm caused to people and relationships as a result of crime or other wrongdoing

Note 1 to entry: Restorative justice is "a victim-centered response to crime that provides opportunities for those most directly affected by the crime—the victim, the offender, their families, and members of the community—to be directly involved in addressing the harm caused by the crime. The restorative justice philosophy is based on (1) values that emphasize the support and involvement of victims and restoring emotional and material losses, (2) holding offenders accountable to the people and communities they violated, (3) providing opportunities for conflict resolution and problem-solving, and (4) strengthening public safety through community-building."

Note 2 to entry: Definition and Note 1 adapted from USLegal.com. [8]

3.45. STUDENT

individual learner in an education abroad *program* (3.40)

3.46. STUDENT AFFAIRS

administrative sector or category of student support services that focuses on supporting student growth and development outside of the classroom

3.47. STUDENT LEARNING AND DEVELOPMENT

growth that is an intended outcome

Note 1 to entry: Student learning and development refers to the changes that result when students are exposed to new experiences, concepts, information, and ideas. The knowledge, understanding, and personal growth are generated, in this context, from interactions with higher education learning environments.

Note 2 to entry: Adapted from the Council for the Advancement of Standards, Glossary of Terms. [7]

3.48. ADDITIONAL TERMS AND DEFINITIONS

These and additional definitions related to the field of education abroad are available in the Glossary published by The Forum on Education Abroad. [11]

4. GUIDING PRINCIPLES

4.1. MISSION AND GOALS

Each organization **shall** write and distribute its mission, goals, objectives, and outcomes.

4.1.1. Each organization **shall** create and distribute a mission statement that defines the scope of its work, values, and aspirations.

4.1.2. Responsible parties **shall** ensure that educational objectives are central to program design and implementation and that the objectives support the mission and goals.

4.1.3. Responsible parties **shall** write and distribute goals, objectives, and outcomes for education abroad programming to partners and participants.

4.1.4. Responsible parties **shall** evaluate the ways in which education abroad programming is or is not achieving its mission, goals, objectives, and outcomes.

4.1.5. Responsible parties **shall** assess the outcomes and use these findings for continuous improvement.

shall = minimum requirement **should** = recommendation **can** = possibility

4.2.   COLLABORATION AND TRANSPARENCY

Collaborations **shall** be equitable and transparent; they **shall** communicate goals and distribution of responsibilities to each responsible party.

4.2.1.   Collaboration **shall** be based on mutual respect and be mutually beneficial.

4.2.2.   Collaborators **shall** discuss and clarify:
- Compatibility of missions and alignment of goals, objectives, and outcomes
- Determining the objectives of the partnership
- Establishing respective financial responsibilities
- Assigning functional roles or tasks to responsible parties
- Establishing policies and procedures
- Managing health, safety, and security risks

4.2.3.   Collaborators **shall** formalize all of the above in writing.

4.2.4.   Collaborators **should** evaluate all of the above for continuous improvement and clarification of responsibilities.

GUIDING PRINCIPLES

4.3. ETHICS

Each organization **shall** collaborate and operate in accordance with ethical principles.

4.3.1. Each organization **shall** adopt the ethical principles and guidelines established by The Forum on Education Abroad or use an internal code of ethics that includes clauses related to all responsible parties involved in conducting education abroad activities.

4.3.2. Each organization **shall** prepare its personnel for ethical decision-making and practices.

4.3.3. Responsible parties **shall** conduct education abroad activities and advise students in an ethically responsible manner.

4.3.4. Responsible parties **shall** adhere to ethical practices in teaching, work, service/ volunteering, and research abroad.

4.3.5. Responsible parties **shall** make participants aware of the ethical implications of their academic work, activities, and interactions abroad.

4.3.6. Each organization **shall** promote respect for the cultures and values of all involved, including the communities from which the participants come and the communities in which they operate.

4.3.7. Each organization **should** consider the social, cultural, economic, and environmental impacts of its education abroad programming.

shall = minimum requirement   **should** = recommendation   **can** = possibility

4.4. EQUITY, DIVERSITY, AND INCLUSION

Each organization **shall** prioritize equity, diversity, and inclusion.

4.4.1.   Each organization **shall** establish equitable and inclusive policies and procedures.

4.4.2.   Each organization **should** emphasize equity, diversity, and inclusion in program design, implementation, goals, objectives, and outcomes.

4.4.3.   Each organization **should** develop structures to examine, identify, and address systemic biases and deficiencies in its policies, practices, and programs.

4.4.4.   Each organization **should** ensure equitable access to education abroad.

4.4.5.   Each organization **shall** establish meaningful contacts and connections with diverse partners, employ and enroll diverse participants, and foster inclusive communities.

4.4.6.   Each organization **should** design its programs to provide opportunities for students to interact with broadly diverse peers, personnel, and members of local communities.

4.4.7.   Responsible parties **should** assess student learning related to portfolio and program learning goals and disaggregate data by student demographics such as gender, socioeconomic status, race, and ethnicity to check for equitable outcomes for all students.

5. ADMINISTRATIVE FRAMEWORK

5.1. POLICIES, PROCEDURES, AND GUIDELINES

Each organization **shall** define policies, procedures, and guidelines (and/or use the Guidelines established by The Forum on Education Abroad) to govern its programs and practices and prepare its personnel to apply them.

5.1.1. Policies, procedures, and guidelines **shall** be inclusive, equitable, transparent, and consistently implemented.

5.1.2. Each organization **shall** periodically conduct reviews to evaluate the application and effectiveness of policies, procedures, and guidelines.

5.1.3. Each organization **shall** have guidelines for program design, including, but not limited to:
- Support for educational objectives
- Relationship of curriculum to stated program goals
- Site-specific learning opportunities

5.1.4. Each organization **shall** have procedures facilitating program administration, including, but not limited to:
- Program proposal and approval process
- Recruitment and student selection
- Collection and analysis of program evaluations; distribution of results
- Regular review of ongoing programs

shall = minimum requirement   **should** = recommendation   **can** = possibility

5.1.5. Each organization **shall** have policies and procedures in place that govern personnel matters, conduct, and training, including, but not limited to:
- Participant conduct management
- Communication protocols
- Participant health, well-being, safety, and security
- Emergency management and response
- Partner relationships, roles, and responsibilities

5.1.6. Each organization **shall** have policies that govern student matters, including:
- Academic affairs: course availability, assessment, credit transfer, grade conversions, grade appeals, research ethics, and academic integrity
- Student affairs: student conduct matters, including, but not limited to, drug and alcohol use, mental health and well-being, culturally-sensitive behavior, sexual misconduct, travel, housing, disciplinary process, and appeal process
- Student finances: financial aid, scholarships, program cost disclosure, payment, cancellation, and reimbursement

5.1.7. Each organization **shall** have policies and procedures in place regarding security and risk management that prioritize the health, well-being, and safety of students and personnel, including, but not limited to:

- Risk assessment and monitoring for program locations and activities
- Tracking, responding to, and reporting critical incidents
- Written emergency plans and protocols
- Insurance coverage

5.1.8. Each organization **should** have guidelines governing its partnerships, including but not limited to:

- Establishing partnerships and formalizing collaboration
- Responsibility for security and risk management
- Managing privacy, confidentiality, and disclosure practices
- Marketing practices
- Partnership review

shall = minimum requirement   **should** = recommendation   **can** = possibility

5.2. FINANCIAL AND HUMAN RESOURCES

Each organization **shall** be fiscally responsible and ensure that each program in its portfolio is funded and staffed to meet its goals.

5.2.1. Each organization **shall** commit to planning, delivery, evaluation, and assessment for continuous improvement.

5.2.2. Personnel involved in all aspects of the program **shall** be equitably remunerated, qualified, and trained for their roles to meet the program objectives for all students.

5.2.2.1. Each responsible party **shall** consider local standards and cost of living when determining a fair and ethical level of remuneration.

5.2.2.2. Each responsible party **shall** invest in training specific to program needs.

5.2.2.3. Each responsible party **should** define "qualified" relative to the program needs, including, but not limited to, consideration of:
- academic qualifications
- professional certifications
- experience

5.2.3. Each organization **shall** ensure workloads that enable personnel to support program goals.

5.2.4. Each organization **shall** provide risk management, preparedness, and emergency response measures for all programs and ensure insurance coverage is in place.

5.2.5. Each organization **shall** facilitate reasonable accommodations to enable students of varying needs and disability status to participate in education abroad.

5.2.6. Responsible parties **should** ensure that facilities and infrastructure, including housing, are suited to the goals of the program.

5.2.7. Responsible parties **shall** provide a safe environment that supports learning for all students.

shall = minimum requirement   **should** = recommendation   **can** = possibility

6. STUDENT LEARNING AND DEVELOPMENT

6.1. BEFORE PROGRAM

Responsible parties **shall** prepare all students to be successful abroad throughout the program design, outreach, advising, application, and pre-departure processes.

> 6.1.1. Responsible parties **shall** keep specific learning outcomes and educational objectives central to program design.

> 6.1.2. Responsible parties **shall** communicate the value of education abroad for students' personal, academic, and career goals.

> 6.1.3. Responsible parties **shall** endeavor to recruit and advise students from all segments of the student population, including those who are historically underserved by their organization's programs.

>> 6.1.3.1. Responsible parties **should** develop strategies to increase participation by historically underserved groups.

> 6.1.4. Responsible parties **shall** communicate the importance of understanding the social, historical, political, economic, linguistic, cultural, and environmental context(s) for each program and location.

> 6.1.5. Responsible parties **shall** prepare students to participate in the curricular and co-curricular aspects of each program.

STUDENT LEARNING

6.1.6.   Responsible parties **shall** engage students in academic planning relevant to their studies and programs, including, but not limited to, consideration of:
- course equivalencies
- credit and credit articulation
- academic differences
- assessment and grading
- relevant career plans

6.1.7.   Responsible parties **shall** evaluate student competencies and place students in language and other courses at their level.

6.1.8.   Responsible parties **shall** communicate expectations for conduct and consequences of behaviors to participants.

6.1.9.   Responsible parties **shall** prepare participants to navigate the cultural transition and to engage in culturally-relevant, ethical, and reciprocally-beneficial activities in relation to the local context.

6.1.9.1.   Responsible parties **should** encourage students to consider the social, cultural, economic, and environmental impact of each program and to mitigate negative or harmful impacts.

6.1.9.2.   Responsible parties **shall** communicate to participants the significance of identities including, but not limited to, racial, ethnic, sexual, gender, religious, ability, citizenship or nationality, and socioeconomic status in relation to the program context.

shall = minimum requirement   **should** = recommendation   **can** = possibility

6.1.10. Responsible parties **shall** provide students with information related to accessing physical, mental, and emotional health and well-being services.

6.1.11. Responsible parties **shall** prepare students to manage their safety by providing resources related to concerns including, but not limited to:
- physical risks
- behavior
- property crime
- liability and legal issues
- sexual misconduct
- identity-based discrimination
- country-specific recommendations

6.1.12. Recognizing that not all countries have in place the same support and infrastructure as the home institution, responsible parties **shall**:
- clearly convey to students the importance of disclosing mental and physical disability status, accommodation, and other specific needs;
- work with other responsible parties and students to determine how their needs may be met on the program;
- and advise students on other program options if their needs cannot be met.

6.1.13.   Responsible parties **shall** publish and provide full program cost estimates to students in writing prior to acceptance.

    6.1.13.1.   Responsible parties **should** provide information on financial topics, including, but not limited to:
- all costs of participation
- financing options
- financial aid
- scholarships
- loans
- budgeting
- currency conversion and exchange rates

    6.1.13.2.   Responsible parties **should** support students in identifying and accessing sources of funding, including competitive scholarships and grants.

6.1.14.   Responsible parties **shall** prepare students to manage program logistics including travel, housing, and group dynamics.

6.1.15.   Responsible parties **shall** communicate the need to obtain passports or alternative travel documents for students of all citizenship statuses.

    6.1.15.1.   Responsible parties **can** support passport and travel document procurement processes.

6.1.16.   Responsible parties **shall** communicate the need to comply with host country immigration and/or visa processes for students of all citizenship statuses.

6.1.16.1.   Responsible parties **should** support the immigration and/or visa processes with information and required documentation.

6.2. DURING PROGRAM

Responsible parties **shall** support student learning and development to achieve portfolio and/or program learning goals.

6.2.1.   Responsible parties **shall** communicate to students their responsibilities for managing program logistics including travel, housing, and group dynamics.

6.2.2.   Responsible parties **shall** communicate expectations for conduct, consequences of behaviors, and appeals processes.

6.2.2.1.   Responsible parties **can** develop strategies to support conduct and behavior improvement, including reflective activities or restorative justice programming.

6.2.3.   Responsible parties **shall** support students' understanding of the social, historical, political, economic, linguistic, cultural, and environmental context(s) for each program and location.

6.2.4.   Responsible parties **shall** support students' participation in the curricular and co-curricular aspects of the program.

    6.2.4.1.   Responsible parties **should** support students in relating the experience to personal career goals.

6.2.5.   Responsible parties **shall** support students to interact in a respectful, ethical, mindful, and sustainable way in the local community.

    6.2.5.1.   Responsible parties **can** provide students with opportunities to reflect on the social, cultural, economic, and environmental impact of their activities.

6.2.6.   Responsible parties **shall** support students as they navigate identities including race, ethnicity, sexuality, gender, religion, ability, and socioeconomic status in the local context.

6.2.7.   Responsible parties **shall** support students in accessing physical, mental, and emotional health and well-being services.

6.2.8.   Responsible parties **shall** support students in managing their safety by providing resources related to concerns including:
- physical risks
- behavior
- property crime
- liability and legal issues
- sexual misconduct
- identity-based discrimination
- communication, social media use, and freedom of expression
- country-specific recommendations

STUDENT LEARNING   **shall** = minimum requirement   **should** = recommendation   **can** = possibility

6.2.9. Responsible parties **shall** support students with accommodation needs related to disability status and identity and determine how their needs may be met in the program.

6.2.10. Responsible parties **shall** support students in obtaining and maintaining legal immigration status or direct them to appropriate resources.

6.3. AFTER PROGRAM

Responsible parties **shall** support post-program integration and application of academic, professional, and personal learning.

6.3.1. Responsible parties **shall** create opportunities for reflection.

6.3.1.1. Responsible parties **can** provide occasions for students to share their experiences through opportunities including panels, photos, videos, essays, and research.

6.3.2. For credit-bearing programs, responsible parties **shall** support students in the course equivalency and credit articulation process.

6.3.3. Responsible parties **should** create opportunities for integration of learning abroad with future learning.

6.3.4. Responsible parties **shall** provide resources related to student mental and physical well-being related to program participation.

STUDENT LEARNING

6.3.5. Responsible parties **should** prepare students to identify transferable skills developed through education abroad.

    6.3.5.1. Responsible parties **should** prepare students to communicate the value of education abroad to employers and other audiences.

    6.3.5.2. Responsible parties **can** offer leadership opportunities or ambassador programs for students.

6.3.6. Responsible parties **should** encourage continuing local and global engagement in culturally-relevant, ethical, and reciprocally-beneficial activities.

    6.3.6.1. Responsible parties **can** work with students to mitigate the social, cultural, economic, and environmental impacts of their travel experiences.

6.3.7. Responsible parties **can** inform students about opportunities to build upon their learning abroad experience, including, but not limited to, academic, governmental, and non-governmental programs, fellowships, and grants.

shall = minimum requirement   **should** = recommendation   **can** = possibility

BIBLIOGRAPHY

[1] *How to write standards.* The International Organization for Standardization, 2016, https://www.iso.org/files/live/sites/isoorg/files/archive/pdf/en/how-to-write-standards.pdf. Accessed 30 Sept 2019.

[2] *Critical Incident Reporting* Policy. North Dakota Department of Health and Human Services, Medical Services Division, 2008, https://www.nd.gov/dhs/info/pubs/mfp/docs/critical-incidents-reporting-policy.pdf. Accessed 30 Sept 2019.

[3] "Making Excellence Inclusive." Association of American Colleges and Universities, 2019, https://www.aacu.org/making-excellence-inclusive. Accessed 30 Sept 2019.

[4] *Oxford Living Dictionaries.* Oxford University Press, 2019, https://en.oxforddictionaries.com/definition. Accessed 30 Sept 2019.

[5] *Cambridge Dictionary.* Cambridge University Press, 2019, https://dictionary.cambridge.org/us/dictionary/english/identity. Accessed 30 Sept 2019.

[6] "Instructional educational institution." UNESCO Institute of Statistics, 2019, http://uis.unesco.org/en/glossary-term/instructional-educational-institution. Accessed 30 Sept 2019.

[7] "Glossary of CAS Terms." Council for the Advancement of Standards, 2019, https://www.cas.edu/glossary. Accessed 30 Sept 2019.

[8] "Post-Secondary Education Law and Legal Definition." *USLegal.com*, 2016, https://definitions.uslegal.com/p/post-secondary-education/. Accessed 30 Sept 2019.

[9] "ISO Terms Definitions." ISO Quality Services Ltd., 2019, https://www.isoqsltd.com/iso-terms-definitions/. Accessed 30 Sept 2019.

[10] Nguyen, D. H. K. "Reasonable Accommodations: What Are They and Who Decides?" *Higher Education Law*, 2016, http://www.highereducationlaw.org/url/2016/7/29/reasonable-accommodations-what-are-they-and-who-decides.html. Accessed 30 Sept 2019.

[11] "Education Abroad Glossary." The Forum on Education Abroad, 2019, https://forumea.org/resources/glossary/. Accessed 30 Sept 2019.

ANNEX: TOPICAL INDEX

ANNEX: TOPICAL INDEX

CODE OF ETHICS FOR EDUCATION ABROAD

Third Edition

THE FORUM
ON EDUCATION ABROAD

1. INTRODUCTION

This document, published by The Forum on Education Abroad, is designed to guide ethical decision-making and assist organizations as they seek to provide education abroad experiences and services in accord with the highest ethical standards. The Shared Values and Principles of Professional Practice outlined below are essential to the fair and just administration of education abroad programs and the welfare of the learners that we serve.

The Forum on Education Abroad is recognized by the US Department of Justice and the Federal Trade Commission as the Standards Development Organization (SDO) for the field of education abroad. This document serves as a normative reference to the *Standards of Good Practice for Education Abroad* (6th edition).

Please refer to the *Standards of Good Practice*, section 3, for definitions of frequently used and field-specific terms.

2. SHARED VALUES

A. RESPONSIBILITY TO LEARNERS

We deliver impactful, accessible, and intellectually and personally meaningful programs that strive to meet the *Standards of Good Practice for Education Abroad*.

We endeavor to share with learners the value and significance of international education and experience, and the impact that it can have on them and those with whom they interact. We encourage learners to maximize international learning and engagement through meaningful and respectful communication with other people and other cultures, and to reflect on and articulate the value and meaning of their experiences.

We recognize the importance of establishing clear expectations and communicating them to learners based on these shared values. We know that empowered and informed learners make responsible decisions, take accountability for their actions, and understand the limits of responsibility.

B. **TRUTHFULNESS AND TRANSPARENCY**

We communicate openly and honestly with all stakeholders, and our interactions with learners and stakeholders are founded in trust. We uphold accuracy and transparency of decision-making, policies, procedures, program promotion, and partnerships. Service to our learners is central to our decision-making and we avoid conflicts of interest that are counter to this goal.

C. **EQUITY, DIVERSITY, AND INCLUSION**

We seek out opportunities to engage with diverse populations and perspectives, and do so with patience, understanding, humility, and respect, modelling the behavior we aim to cultivate in our learners. We endeavor to expand access to education abroad, and to create an environment of inclusivity that is open, respectful, and safe for all. We strive for equity in our treatment of all. We do not accept intolerance, and we work to eliminate inequities within our organizations and communities.

D. **RECIPROCITY AND RESPECT FOR OTHERS**

Reciprocity must be valued as we consider the consequences of our activity on a global scale with respect to the environment, economies, communities, and cultures. We are sensitive to dynamics of power and privilege and the impact of our actions in the communities in which we operate and with whom we engage.

We work to ensure that our interactions and interrelationships with the communities in which we operate, whether in-country or virtually, are mutually beneficial. Our work with learners, host communities, and internal stakeholders at our institutions and external partners is grounded in reciprocity.

3. PRINCIPLES OF PROFESSIONAL PRACTICE

A. EDUCATIONAL QUALITY

Our educational content, assessment, and policies foster an environment which prioritizes student learning and academic excellence.

B. ADVOCACY

We advocate for the value of enhanced global perspectives and intercultural understanding through global learning. Wherever possible, we promote The Forum's mission, which is to "cultivate educators who champion high quality education abroad experiences that ignite curiosity, impact lives, and contribute to a better world."

C. HEALTH, SAFETY, AND WELL-BEING

We are committed to the personal safety, health, and well-being of our participants and local partners. We assess risks and endeavor to establish and maintain programs that support the emotional, intellectual, and physical safety of our participants. We orient our participants and provide them with detailed information about health and safety risks in host environments as well as available support services. We have plans and training to respond to emergencies that may impact our participants.

D. PRICING AND AFFORDABILITY

We work to the best of our ability to develop and operate global learning opportunities that provide accessible, affordable opportunities while maintaining quality of offerings and learner support. Our pricing is transparent, and financial policies are clear, equitable, and consistently implemented. We retain provisions for handling emergencies and sufficient financial resources to meet the obligations of each program.

E. PARTNERSHIPS

We pursue business relationships that are mutually beneficial and respectful of each other's goals, principles, and values. We endeavor to establish partnerships that are fair, just, and equitable, and are sensitive to power differentials between organizations. Our interactions with partners are collegial, transparent, mindful of intellectual property rights, avoid conflicts of interest, and put learners first.

F. PRIVACY AND CONFIDENTIALITY

We respect and protect the privacy and confidentiality of participants, personnel, partners, and stakeholders in our work in compliance with applicable privacy laws and policies. We communicate limitations of confidentiality promptly and clearly.

G. RESPECT FOR LOCAL LAWS AND CULTURES

We operate our programs with respect to local customs and cultural norms, and ensure that all participants in those programs are informed and similarly respectful. We acknowledge our collective responsibility to conduct education abroad programs in accordance with governing laws. We aspire to ethical behavior above and beyond what is required by law.

H. SUSTAINABILITY

We seek to wed sustainable environmental practices with our academic and programmatic goals. In doing so, we acknowledge that sustainable actions are reached through informed and balanced decision-making and can have positive effects on relationships, the economic welfare of all, cultural traditions, and the global environment. We consider the impact of our work on the environment as well as the economics and cultures of host communities.

I. ACCOUNTABILITY AND CONTINUOUS IMPROVEMENT

We take accountability for our actions, decisions, and for their consequences. We are accountable to our learners for the education they receive. We continuously make improvements to our programming and practices to benefit participants, stakeholders, and the communities in which we operate.

FOUR QUESTIONS TO GUIDE ETHICAL DECISION-MAKING IN EDUCATION ABROAD

- Is it in the best interests of the learners, their growth and well-being?

- Is it truthful, fair, transparent?

- Is it equitable and inclusive?

- Is it grounded in reciprocity? Do the host communities agree?

ADDITIONAL RESOURCES

Guidance on Program Site Visits

Guidance on Conflicts of Interest

Guidelines for Community Engagement, Service-Learning, and Volunteer Experiences Abroad

Guidelines for Good Business Partnerships

Guidelines for Internships Abroad

Guidelines for Undergraduate Research, Field Studies, and Independent Study Projects Abroad

ACKNOWLEDGEMENTS

The Forum thanks the Code of Ethics Working Group for their contribution to the preparation of these Guidelines:

Brian Brubaker, The Pennsylvania State University, chair
Mark Eckman, University of Massachusetts Amherst
Elizabeth Frohlich, The Forum on Education Abroad
Julie Leitman, Academic Programs International (API)
Gina Lopardo, Seattle University
Kate Manni, The Pennsylvania State University
Mary Ogburn, AUIP (American Universities International Programs Ltd.)
Anthony Ogden, Gateway International Group
David Shallenberger, SIT Graduate Institute
Michael Steinberg, IES Abroad
Sarah Westmoreland, University of Colorado Boulder

The Forum also thanks the members of our community who shared their feedback and suggestions during the public comment period.

Pressing
RESET
— for —
Efficient Mountain Biking

original
strength

Contributor: Michael Barnard

ISBN: 979-8-9865860-1-4 (Paperback)

OS Press

Original Strength for Mountain Biking

Mountain biking is a lifelong sport that almost anyone can enjoy. From kids to adults, mountain biking is a great way to challenge yourself and enjoy the outdoors. Whether it's the tough climbs, a fast and thrilling descent or just enjoying the views, mountain biking offers fun for all.

Strength and moving well are two necessary components for every rider. These help you with your endurance so you can ride stronger for longer, assist in injury prevention and improve your longevity in the sport. Mountain biking requires the rider to use certain body positions and powerful movements - from hinging deep into an attack position, producing enough tension to grind up a steep climb, absorbing impact from jumps and drops, to exploding into a bunny hop to clear an obstacle. When you are mountain biking, you want your body ready and able to execute the necessary skills.

However, our modern lifestyle tends to lack a variety of movements. Since many of our daily positions mirror our biking position - from sitting at the desk or while we drive with our hips hinged at 90 degrees and being slightly bent over - this can leave many avid riders with issues like low back pain, underactive glutes, a weak core, and even inefficient control of their breathing.

To help undo these effects, we need to Press RESET on our body to restore our posture and movement quality - in other words, restore our original strength. Your original strength is what allows you to live life the way you want to. It is having the ability to participate in whatever activities you want, while doing them safely and confidently. When you have your original strength, your body is moving in an optimal way and free to express its full potential.

Pressing RESET on your body will result in moving well and enhancing your strength. This allows you to access the body positions necessary to mountain bike, giving you potential to execute the skills you need on the bike. It will also help restore poor posture and muscle imbalances, which we often get from not balancing our time off the bike with quality movement practice.

In this booklet, we will share RESETs that get your body to move optimally so you can ride and feel your best. Are you ready to unlock your movement and riding potential?

Pressing RESET

By engaging in RESET movements, your body will begin to restore and build back its original strength.

These movements are based on the three pillars of human movement.

1. Breathe with the diaphragm (belly breathe)
2. Activate the vestibular system (balance and proprioceptive system)
3. Engage in contra-lateral movement (gait pattern, crawling, walking)

These are the same things you did as a baby and child when developing your ability to move and explore your world; they are just as valuable today. They are embedded in the movement programs of our nervous system. That is, we are designed to do them throughout life and it is natural for us to use these movements each day. These movements are gentle, accessible and highly effective at restoring and rebuilding your movement and strength.

Moving well allows you to access the needed body positions, as well as enhance your strength, to execute the skills required to mountain bike. It will also help restore poor posture and muscle imbalances, which we often get from not balancing our time off the bike with quality movement practice. When we engage in these reset movements, our brains build new and restore old neural connections; which leads to a healthier body.

In this booklet are Resets that can help your body move optimally so you can ride and feel your best. The Resets in this book will help you unlock your movement to unlock your riding potential.

The Big Five RESETs

Following the three pillars of human movement, in Original Strength we Press RESET by focusing on five developmental movements. These developmental movements are inspired by the very movements that each of us did as babies to develop strength, balance and coordination.

These movements are:

1. Diaphragmatic Breathing
2. Head Control
3. Rolling
4. Rocking
5. Crawling, or contra-lateral, midline crossing movements.

These five movements, and their variations, are at the heart of the nervous system's design. They are familiar to the body and establish and restore the body's "reflexive strength".

Pressing
RESET

Breathing with the Diaphragm

- The secret to breathing efficiency

Why?

- Breathing with the chest is inefficient and doesn't let you use full lung capacity.
- Strengthening the diaphragm allows you to pull more air into your lungs, which can provide more oxygen to the working muscles.
- The diaphragm is a spinal stabilizer and it helps protect your spine. Proper diaphragmatic breathing allows you to move well.
- Breathing with the diaphragm calms your nervous system.
- You were born a belly breather.

Movement #1

BELLY BREATHING

- Lie on your back, with legs outstretched and hands on belly.Or with feet up and knees pulled in.
- Place your tongue on the roof of your mouth and close your lips.
- Breathe in and out of your nose, pulling air deep into your belly.

Movement #2

SHORT POSITION, HANDS AND KNEES

- Kneel on the floor with your hands on the floor in front of your knees.
- Place your tongue on the roof of your mouth and close your lips.
- Breathe in and out of your nose, pulling air deep into your belly.

Head Control

Why?

- When you keep your head up, you can look further down the trail.

- Strengthens your neck to maintain proper head position in rough sections of the trail and helps keep your head and chest square when cornering.

- Controlling the movements of your head activates your vestibular system and improves its function.

- Every muscle in your body is reflexively wired to the movements of your head.

- Head control is essential to health and strength throughout your lifetime.

Movement #1

QUADRUPED HEAD NOD

- Kneel on the floor with your hands on the floor in front of your knees.

- Place your tongue on the roof of your mouth and close your lips.

- Perform head nods by raising and lowering your head as far as your neck will allow pain-free.

- Lead the movement with your eyes.

- Do not hold your breath; continue breathing through your nose.

Movement #2

QUADRUPED HEAD ROTATIONS

- Kneel on the floor, allowing your butt to rest on your legs with your hands on the floor in front of your knees.

- Place your tongue on the roof of your mouth and close your lips.

- Rotate your head left and right as if looking at your back pockets.

- Lead the movement with your eyes.

- Do not drop your head; look over your shoulders.

- Do not hold your breath; continue breathing through your nose.

Reset #3

Rolling

Why?

- Mobilizes and opens the spine and hips from sitting too much

- Allows you to access more power on the bike because you're not fighting stiff muscles or joints, you will move more fluidly on the bike.

- Reduces back pain.

- Rolling connects your shoulders to your hips.

Movement #1

UPPER BODY HALF ROLL

- Lie on your belly with your arms overhead.
- Place your tongue on the roof of your mouth.
- Bend your right elbow, look at it, and reach for the floor behind you. Try to touch the floor with your elbow.

Movement #2

WINDSHIELD WIPER

- Lie on your back and place your arms perpendicular to your torso.
- Bend your knees toward your chest to lift your tailbone off the floor. Your feet will be in the air.
- Place your tongue on the roof of your mouth and close your lips.
- While keeping your shoulder blades in contact with the ground, rotate your legs from side to side.
- Keep your knees pulled up toward your chest as you rotate your legs to the side. Do not let them drift away.

Reset #4

Rocking

Why?

- Integrates all the joints of the body into one whole body.
- Helps coordinate movement for jumps and impacts.
- Develops your hip hinge for explosive movements.
- Coordinates the shoulders and the hips.
- Helps mobilize stiff ankle joints.
- Restores posture.

Movement #1

ROCKING ON HANDS AND KNEES

- Kneel on the floor with your hands on the floor in front of your knees.
- Place your tongue on the roof of your mouth.
- Hold your head up and keep your eyes on the horizon.
- Rock back and forth, shifting your weight over your hands and then back over your feet.
- Keep your back flat. Do not let it round or bow up.
- Feet can be plantarflexed or dorsiflexed.

Movement #2

ADDUCTOR ROCKING

- Get on your hands and knees with your hands on the floor in front of your knees.

- Place your tongue on the roof of your mouth.

- Hold your head up, keeping your eyes on the horizon.

- Extend your right leg out to the side.

- Gently rock back and forth, shifting your weight over your hands and back over your feet.

- Repeat with your left leg extended out to the side.

- Explore this gently.

Reset #5

Crawling

- The secret to high tension efficiency

Why?

- It helps dial your tension meter to produce the right amount when needed.
- Helps you recover faster after those high-tension efforts.
- Restores proper core function.
- Restores contra-lateral movement pattern. Crawling connects both halves of the brain.
- Reflexively ties your body together and strengthens reflexes so the body can move more gracefully and powerfully.
- It strengthens the nervous system.

Movement #1

SPEED SKATERS

- Get on your hands and knees as if in a crawling position. Keep your back flat.
- Place your tongue on the roof of your mouth.
- Hold your head up and keep your eyes on the horizon.
- Move your opposite arm and leg back together.
- This will wake up your backside.

Movement #2

HANDS AND KNEES CRAWLING

- Get on your hands and knees in a crawling position, keep your back flat.
- Place your tongue on the roof of your mouth.
- Hold your head up and keep your eyes on the horizon.
- Move your opposite arms and legs together and crawl forward or backward.

Movement #3

LEOPARD CRAWLING

- Get on your hands and feet, down in a crawl position, but keep your knees lifted slightly from the ground and your back flat.
- Place your tongue on the roof of your mouth.
- Hold your head up and keep your eyes on the horizon.
- Keep your butt down below your head.
- Move your opposite arms and legs together and crawl forward or backward.

Movement #4

CROSS CRAWLS

- Standing position
- Place your tongue on the roof of your mouth and close your lips.
- Touch opposite limbs together.
- You can touch your left hand to right thigh, right elbow to left knee, etc.

Movement #5

DEAD BUGS

- Lie on your back with your arms and legs outstretched.
- Place your tongue on the roof of your mouth and close your lips.
- Extend your arms and legs above you and towards the sky.
- Lower your right arm behind your head and lower your left leg to just above the floor.
- Once lowered, bring them back to the starting position and repeat with the opposing limbs.
- Only move two limbs at a time.

Your
DESIGN

The Power in Your Design

The landscape challenges on the mountain bike trail require the rider to:

- Perform a variety of body positions
- Produce high amounts of tension
- Recover in time for the next obstacle.

This can seem like a daunting task, but it doesn't have to be. With a little focus on your movement, you can get the most out of every ride and feel good at the end.

There is power in your design. When you engage in your design, your body remains strong, healthy and regulated. Using the RESETs to tap back into your original strength, you'll ride with more focus, control and strength and recover faster. You'll have the ability to ride longer and with more confidence. Your newfound abilities will have you enjoying the trail more than ever.

Connecting RESETs to the Trail:

The five RESETs can be used to specifically get you ready for the trail.

Diaphragmatic Breathing

While lying in a comfortable position on your back or hands and knees for 1-2 minutes, breathe through your nose.

This is a great time to start focusing on the ride and preparing your mind and body. Closing your eyes can allow you to visualize your ride, which can be very powerful. Even during your ride, learning to breathe with your diaphragm will help you recover faster and stay more focused.

Head Nods/Rotations

In the quadruped or Rocking position, perform head nods and rotations for 1-2 minutes. Explore this gently, do not move into pain.

Head nods/rotations will start to strengthen the muscles in your neck. Improving your ability to keep your head up and eyes on the horizon allows you to see further down the trail. Proper head control is important for keeping your head and chest square during cornering.

Upper Body Half Rolls

Lying on your stomach, reach with your right elbow and try to touch the floor. Repeat this for the left elbow for 1-2 minutes.

Rolling like this will loosen up your upper back and spine. Rolling will help you get in those dynamic positions on the bike needed for cornering or riding steep terrain. It will also relieve tension in the upper back from holding on to the handlebars too tight.

Windshield Wipers

While lying on your back for 1-2 minutes, move your legs back and forth to each side.

These mobilize the lower lumbar area. Lumbar mobilization is needed to help get the hips into a good position for cornering on the trail. It also greatly helps to relieve the lower back pain that many riders get.

Rocking

On hands and knees, begin rocking back and forth for 1-2 minutes.

This will prepare the whole body for getting into a low-hinged attack position for tackling all the obstacles on the trail. It improves coordination between the hips and shoulders to learn how to take the impacts on the trail or use explosive movements to get over certain obstacles.

Adductor Rocking

On hands and knees with one leg extended to the side, rock back and forth for 1-2 minutes.

This is a great movement for releasing adductor muscles that tend to tighten up from all the pedaling. This will allow greater ease of motion both on and off the bike.

Speed Skaters

On hands and knees, raise, and move your opposite arm and leg back together for 1-2 minutes.

This movement will gently move the shoulder into extension that it doesn't always get. By bringing the leg back the glute will gently fire up and begin to strengthen. This will reduce back pain and also improve overall trail strength, especially when standing pedaling.

Crawling

On hands and knees, or hands and feet. Begin moving opposite limbs together to crawl forward or backward for 1-2 minutes.

This may take your riding to the next level. This movement will tie the whole body together and build a very strong body. This is great for those high-tension efforts on the trail, such as steep punchy climbs or rocks and roots obstacles. Crawling will teach your mind and body how to handle those efforts and recover quickly for the next one.

Cross Crawls

Stand up and touch opposite limbs together for 1-2 minutes.

Cross crawls improve your focus and coordination. They will gently prepare your glute, hip and core muscles for the trail.

Dead Bugs

Lying on your back with all your limbs up, lower two opposing limbs to the floor and back up for one minute. Then repeat with the other two for another minute.

Dead bugs will strengthen the core muscles of the body as well as the hip flexor muscles. This will help you hold a strong seated or standing pedaling position for longer. Even as you start to fatigue, you won't find yourself draping over the handlebars anymore.

Putting It All Together

Sample pre-ride/everyday RESET Routine

Perform each movement for 1-2 minutes

- Diaphragmatic breathing
- Head Nods/Rotations
- Upper Body Half Rolls
- Windshield Wipers
- Rocking
- Adductor Rocking
- Cross Crawls

This routine works great for a post-ride RESET to jump-start recovery. You can also do it in reverse order.

Sample Training Session

This will help you build your trail strength to ride stronger with fewer aches and pains. You can do this training routine 2-3 times a week along with the pre-ride routine to restore and rebuild your original strength.

Using your body weight, alternate between the two movements for the set time. No need to rush through these; focus on moving well and building strength.

5 Minutes
1A - Squat x 10 reps
1B - Push-Up x 5 reps

Rest 1-2 Minutes, Reset the timer

5 Minutes
2A - Dead Bugs x 10 reps
2B - Speed Skaters x 10 reps

Rest 1-2 Minutes

Crawl x 5 minutes (hands and knees and/or leopard crawling).

Only Got Three Minutes?

Try this super fast RESET whenever you're in a pinch for time.

- Diaphragmatic breathing for 1 minute
  - » Lie down, tongue on the roof of your mouth, close your lips, and breathe.

- Rock on hands and knees for 1 minute
  - » Get on hands and knees, tongue on the roof of your mouth, close your lips, shift your weight forward and back.
- Cross crawls for 1 minute
  - » Tongue on the roof of your mouth, close your lips and touch opposite limbs.

Implementing simple RESET routines will have you riding stronger than ever! Simple RESETs only take a few minutes a day and can immediately improve your body and mind connection and movements. .

Now go ride!

Want to learn more?

This booklet was designed to give a brief overview of the Original Strength System and how it can help you Press RESET on your bike riding.

We put it together because we know it can help everyone and anyone. If you do nothing more than what is in this booklet, you will notice many changes in how your mind and body begin to feel and react to various situations.

Original Strength is a human movement education company with a mission to bring the hope and strength of movement to everybody in the world. Based on the human developmental sequence and the design of the human body, the Original Strength System teaches

movements that help RESET an individual's neuromuscular system allowing them to enjoy improved physical movement and physiological function.

We conduct courses, training, and certifying coaches and instructors. We also develop educational materials for PE teachers, physical therapy students, medical professionals, fitness/health/wellness instructors, sports conditioning professionals, and individuals/groups working with vestibular and neuromuscular functionality.

If you want to know more about Pressing RESET and regaining your original strength, visit https://originalstrength.net. There you will find a variety of books, free video tutorials (OS Movement Snax), and a complete listing of our courses and OS Certified Professionals near you.

You may want to consider finding an OS Certified Professional. These professionals will conduct an Original Strength Screen and Assessment (OSSA), which is the quickest and easiest way to identify areas your movement system needs to go from good to best. The OSSA allows a pro to pinpoint the best place for you to start Pressing RESET and restoring your Original Strength.

We encourage you to reach out to the OS team with any questions you may have.

Press RESET now and live life better &
stronger because you were awesomely
and wonderfully made to accomplish
amazing things.

For more information:

óriginal
strength

Original Strength Systems, LLC
OriginalStrength.net

PressingRESETfor@Originalstrength.net

"... I am fearfully and wonderfully made..."
Psalm 139:14

original
strength

originalstrength.net

Published by

OS PRESS